21st Century
Basic Skills
Library

WHAT DO PEOPLE DO IN WINTER?

by Rebecca Felix

Cherry Lake Publishing • Ann Arbor, Michigan

1

What Do You See?

What kind of game is this family playing?

Keeping Warm

Winter is cold. People find ways to stay warm. They spend more time inside.

People wear warm clothes. They are especially needed outdoors.

Winter Chores

Winter brings snow and ice. People **shovel**. They **scrape** ice from cars.

What Do You See?

What is the carrot for?

Snow Fun

People have fun in snow, too. Jax plays in snow. He makes a snowman.

Jen and Eve sled. They fly down a hill!

Sports

Many people snowboard or ski. They ride a **chairlift**.

Many people ride **snowmobiles** in winter.

What Do You See?

What is Cash skating on?

Cash likes to go ice skating.
He plays hockey.

Soon, spring arrives. What do people do in spring?

Find Out More

BOOK

Glaser, Linda. *It's Winter!* Brookfield, CT: Millbrook, 2002.

WEB SITE

Winter Sports—KidsHealth

kidshealth.org/kid/watch/out/winter_sports.html
Listen to your computer read to you about winter sports
and safety.

Glossary

chairlift (CHAIR-lift) moving seats that hang from a cable and
carry people up or down a mountain

scrape (SKRAPE) to remove ice from something by rubbing it
with a hard tool

shovel (SHUV-ul) using a handheld tool to clear snow

snowmobiles (SNO-moh-beelz) vehicles with skis that are
used to travel over snow

Home and School Connection

Use this list of words from the book to help your child become a better reader. Word games and writing activities can help beginning readers reinforce literacy skills.

arrives	fly	needed	snowman
brings	fun	outdoors	snowmobiles
carrot	games	people	spend
cars	hill	plays	sports
chairlift	hockey	ride	spring
chores	ice	scrape	stay
clothes	ice skating	shovel	time
cold	inside	ski	warm
especially	keeping	sled	ways
family	likes	snow	wear
find	makes	snowboard	winter

What Do You See?

What Do You See? is a feature paired with select photos in this book. It encourages young readers to interact with visual images in order to build the ability to integrate content in various media formats.

You can help your child further evaluate photos in this book with additional activities. Look at the images in the book without the What Do You See? feature. Ask your child to describe one detail in each image, such as a food, activity, or setting.

Index

About the Author

Rebecca Felix is an editor and writer from Minnesota. She likes to go ice skating there in winter. Rebecca also sleds in the snow. But she does not like to shovel the snow!